We hope this book has been informative and helpful on your journey to understanding and celebrating older adults. Thank you for your interest and support!

AF482817

Title: The Masterful Minds of Football

Subtitle: Understanding the Coaching Philosophies of Three Iconic Managers

Series: The Masterminds of Football: Biographies & Memoirs

By Chester Madison

"The most important thing is to win, not just to play good football."
Pep Guardiola, Manchester City Manager

"If you want to be a champion, you have to score more goals than the opponent."
Jose Mourinho, AS Roma Manager

"It's not just about winning, it's about winning with style."
Arsène Wenger, Former Arsenal Manager

"The difference between a successful person and others is not a lack of strength, not a lack of knowledge, but rather a lack of will."
Vince Lombardi, Former American Football Coach (this quote is often used in football as well)

"In football, the result is an impostor. You can do things really, really well but not win. There's something greater than the result, more lasting - a legacy."
Xavi, Former Barcelona Midfielder

"The ball is the most important thing. It's the only thing that never gets tired."
Jürgen Klopp, Liverpool Manager

"I don't believe skill was, or ever will be, the result of coaches. It is a result of a love affair between the child and the ball."
Roy Keane, Former Manchester United Midfielder

"Football is not just about winning, it's about playing with passion and giving your best every time you step onto the pitch."
Diego Simeone, Atlético Madrid Manager

Table of Contents

Introduction

Brief overview of the careers of Ivic, Lippi, and Trapattoni

Football has produced countless legends and heroes over the years, but few have left a mark quite like Tomislav Ivic, Marcello Lippi, and Giovanni Trapattoni. These three coaches share an incredible legacy that spans decades, continents, and some of the biggest clubs and national teams in football history. From Ivic's tactical innovations to Lippi's adaptability and Trapattoni's leadership, these masterful minds of football have transformed the sport and inspired countless players and coaches in their wake.

Tomislav Ivic was born in 1933 in Croatia and began his playing career as a defender for his local club, Hajduk Split. After several years on the pitch, Ivic transitioned to coaching in 1963 and quickly rose to prominence thanks to his innovative tactical ideas and attention to detail. Ivic's first major success came in 1967, when he led his former club, Hajduk Split, to the Yugoslav First League title. From there, Ivic's career took him to some of Europe's top clubs, including Ajax, Anderlecht, and Porto, where he won several league titles and European trophies. Ivic's tactical innovations, such as the "four-man defense" and the "pressing game," have had a lasting impact on football and influenced many of the game's top coaches today.

Marcello Lippi was born in 1948 in Italy and started his playing career as a striker for Sampdoria. After a brief stint as a lower-league coach, Lippi took over at Serie A club Napoli in 1989 and led them to a UEFA Cup victory in 1990. Lippi's success continued at Juventus, where he won five Serie A titles, a Champions League title, and several other domestic and European trophies. Lippi's tactical flexibility and adaptability made him a sought-after coach around the world, and he went on to manage several national teams, including Italy, China, and the United Arab Emirates.

Giovanni Trapattoni was born in 1939 in Italy and started his playing career as a midfielder for Milan. After a successful playing career, Trapattoni transitioned to coaching in the early 1970s and quickly made a name for himself at Milan, where he won two Serie A titles and a European Cup. Trapattoni's success continued at Juventus, where he won six Serie A titles, a European Cup, and several other domestic and European trophies. Trapattoni's leadership and motivational skills were legendary, and he went on to manage several national teams, including Italy, Austria, and the Republic of Ireland.

These three managers represent some of the best and most innovative football minds in history, and their contributions to the sport cannot be overstated. Throughout the rest of this book, we will delve deeper into their careers, exploring their successes, challenges, innovations, and legacies.

Significance of their contributions to football

The impact of Tomislav Ivic, Marcello Lippi, and Giovanni Trapattoni on football is immeasurable. From revolutionizing tactics to inspiring generations of players and coaches, these three masterful minds of football have left a lasting legacy that continues to shape the sport today.

Tomislav Ivic's impact on football can be seen in the tactical innovations he introduced throughout his coaching career. From the "four-man defense" to the "pressing game," Ivic's ideas changed the way teams approached the game and influenced many of the game's top coaches today. Ivic's emphasis on attention to detail and analysis also helped raise the standards of coaching and scouting in football.

Marcello Lippi's contribution to football is his adaptability and tactical flexibility. Lippi was able to successfully manage both club and national teams, winning numerous titles and trophies along the way. Lippi's ability to change tactics mid-game and adapt to his opponents' strengths made him a formidable opponent for any team. Lippi's focus on player psychology and motivation also helped him get the best out of his players and inspire them to greatness.

Giovanni Trapattoni's leadership and motivational skills have made him a legendary figure in football.

Trapattoni's ability to inspire and motivate his players, both on and off the pitch, helped him achieve great success at both club and international level. Trapattoni's tactical innovations, such as the "catenaccio" defense, also had a lasting impact on the game and influenced many coaches to this day.

Overall, the significance of Ivic, Lippi, and Trapattoni's contributions to football is clear. Their innovations, adaptability, leadership, and motivational skills have transformed the sport and inspired countless players and coaches around the world. Throughout the rest of this book, we will explore their careers in more detail, examining their successes, challenges, and legacies, and uncovering the secrets to their incredible impact on football.

The commonalities and differences in their managerial styles

While Tomislav Ivic, Marcello Lippi, and Giovanni Trapattoni all achieved great success as football coaches, their approaches to management varied significantly. Each manager had their unique strengths, weaknesses, and philosophies, which shaped their managerial styles and impacted their teams' performances.

In this section of the book, we will examine the commonalities and differences in the managerial styles of Ivic, Lippi, and Trapattoni, and explore how these styles influenced their teams' success. We will look at factors such as their tactical approaches, communication skills, leadership styles, and approaches to player development, among others.

Despite their differences, there are several commonalities in the managerial styles of Ivic, Lippi, and Trapattoni. All three managers believed in the importance of discipline and organization. They also placed a strong emphasis on analyzing their opponents and tailoring their tactics accordingly.

At the same time, there were significant differences in their approaches to management. Ivic, for example, was known for his meticulous attention to detail and analysis, while Lippi was known for his adaptability and willingness to change tactics mid-game. Trapattoni, meanwhile, was famous for his motivational skills and ability to inspire his players to greatness.

As we delve deeper into the careers of Ivic, Lippi, and Trapattoni, we will explore these similarities and differences in more detail. We will examine their tactical innovations, communication styles, leadership qualities, and their impact on player development. By understanding the unique qualities and managerial styles of these three masterful minds of football, we can gain valuable insights into the art of coaching and the factors that contribute to success in the sport.

The impact they had on the clubs and national teams they managed

Tomislav Ivic, Marcello Lippi, and Giovanni Trapattoni are renowned for their exceptional abilities as football coaches. Over the course of their careers, they achieved great success at the highest levels of the sport, leading some of the most prominent clubs and national teams to glory.

In this section of the book, we will explore the impact that Ivic, Lippi, and Trapattoni had on the clubs and national teams they managed. We will examine the strategies they employed, the players they worked with, and the outcomes they achieved, providing insight into their approach to management and the reasons for their success.

We will begin by examining the clubs that Ivic, Lippi, and Trapattoni managed, analyzing the impact that they had on these teams' performance. Ivic, for example, enjoyed success at a number of top European clubs, including Ajax, Porto, and Atletico Madrid. He implemented his trademark discipline and tactical innovation to great effect, transforming underperforming teams into title contenders.

Lippi, meanwhile, managed several of Italy's most prominent clubs, including Juventus, AC Milan, and Inter Milan. He was known for his tactical flexibility and ability to adapt to changing circumstances, which allowed him to lead his teams to numerous domestic and international titles.

Trapattoni, too, achieved great success at the club level, managing some of Italy and Germany's most successful teams. His motivational skills and tactical acumen helped him to lead his teams to numerous domestic and international titles, including a UEFA Cup and two Bundesliga titles with Bayern Munich.

We will also examine the impact that Ivic, Lippi, and Trapattoni had on the national teams they managed. Ivic, for example, managed the national teams of Croatia, Belgium, and Iran, leading Croatia to the quarter-finals of the 1996 European Championship. Lippi, meanwhile, led Italy to victory in the 2006 World Cup, while Trapattoni managed the national teams of Italy, Portugal, and the Republic of Ireland.

By examining the impact that Ivic, Lippi, and Trapattoni had on the clubs and national teams they managed, we can gain a deeper understanding of their managerial styles and the factors that contributed to their success. We can also gain valuable insights into the art of coaching and the qualities that are required to achieve success at the highest levels of the sport.

Chapter 1: Tomislav Ivic
Early life and playing career

Tomislav Ivic was born on June 30, 1933, in Split, Croatia, which was then part of Yugoslavia. He grew up in a football-loving family and began playing the sport at a young age. Ivic showed great promise as a player and was soon noticed by local coaches for his technical ability and vision on the pitch.

Ivic began his professional playing career at RNK Split, a local football club in his hometown. He quickly established himself as a key player, impressing fans and teammates alike with his technical ability and tactical awareness. His performances attracted the attention of larger clubs, and in 1957 he was signed by Dinamo Zagreb, one of the most successful clubs in Yugoslavia.

At Dinamo Zagreb, Ivic continued to develop his game, playing alongside some of the best players in the country. He established himself as a versatile and intelligent player, capable of playing in several positions on the pitch. Ivic's skill and versatility helped him to win several domestic titles with Dinamo Zagreb, including the Yugoslav Cup in 1960 and the Yugoslav First League in 1962.

In 1962, Ivic was selected to play for the Yugoslavian national team. He made his debut in a friendly match against

Greece, and soon became a regular member of the squad. Ivic played a key role in Yugoslavia's qualification for the 1962 FIFA World Cup in Chile, where they finished fourth.

Throughout his playing career, Ivic was known for his intelligence, tactical awareness, and technical ability. He was respected by his peers and coaches alike, and was widely regarded as one of the best players of his generation.

However, Ivic's playing career was cut short by injury in 1963, at the age of 30. Despite this setback, he remained involved in football, taking on coaching roles at several clubs in Yugoslavia. In 1968, Ivic was appointed as the head coach of Dinamo Zagreb, where he began to make a name for himself as a talented and innovative coach.

Overall, Ivic's early life and playing career provided him with the foundation he needed to succeed as a football coach. His technical ability, tactical awareness, and intelligence on the pitch helped him to develop a deep understanding of the game, which he would later apply to great effect as a coach.

Tomislav Ivic's interest in coaching emerged early on in his playing career. As a player, he was known for his tactical awareness and leadership skills, which laid the foundation for his future success as a coach.

After retiring from playing football in the mid-1960s, Ivic quickly transitioned to coaching. He started his coaching career with local club NK Osijek in Croatia, where he was given full control of the first team at the age of just 25.

Under Ivic's guidance, NK Osijek achieved promotion to the Yugoslav First League, which was a major achievement for a small club with limited resources. This success caught the attention of Hajduk Split, one of Croatia's most prestigious clubs, who appointed Ivic as their head coach in 1970.

At Hajduk Split, Ivic continued to impress with his tactical innovations and player management skills. He introduced new training methods and modernized the club's playing style, which led to a period of sustained success. In his first season, he led Hajduk Split to the Yugoslav Cup and the Yugoslav First League title, a remarkable achievement for a relatively inexperienced coach.

Ivic's success with Hajduk Split caught the attention of other clubs across Europe, and he soon became known as one of the most promising young coaches in the game. In 1974, he was appointed as the head coach of Standard Liege in Belgium, where he won the Belgian First Division title in his first season.

This success led to further opportunities in Europe's top leagues, and Ivic went on to manage some of the biggest clubs in the world, including Ajax Amsterdam, FC Porto, and Atletico Madrid. At each club, he brought his unique approach to coaching, which emphasized tactical flexibility and player development.

Ivic's innovative approach to coaching and player management helped him rise to prominence in the football world, and his success paved the way for future generations of coaches to follow in his footsteps. He passed away in 2011 at the age of 77, but his legacy in football continues to inspire coaches and players around the world.

Tomislav Ivic had an illustrious career as a football coach, spanning over three decades. He managed clubs in several countries and won numerous domestic and international titles. Here are some of his key achievements and success stories:

1. Yugoslavia National Team (1978-1980) Tomislav Ivic's first major success as a coach came with the Yugoslavia national team. He took over the reins in 1978 and led the team to the 1980 European Championship in Italy. The team played an attacking brand of football and was unbeaten throughout the tournament, eventually finishing as runners-up after losing to West Germany in the final.

2. Hajduk Split (1980-1982) Ivic's next challenge was at Hajduk Split, one of the biggest clubs in Croatia. He led them to two consecutive domestic league titles, in 1981 and 1982. The team played a high-tempo, attacking style of football that thrilled the fans and made them one of the most feared teams in Europe.

3. Anderlecht (1982-1983) After his success with Hajduk Split, Ivic moved to Belgium to manage Anderlecht. In his first season, he led the team to the Belgian league title, and also reached the quarter-finals of the UEFA Cup.

However, he left the club at the end of the season due to disagreements with the board.

4. Porto (1984-1986) Ivic's next stop was Portugal, where he managed FC Porto. He won the league title in his first season, and also guided the team to the final of the European Cup, where they lost to Steaua Bucharest on penalties. The following season, he won the league title again and also the Portuguese Cup.

5. Marseille (1986-1987) Ivic's success at Porto earned him a move to French giants Marseille. He took over a team that had not won the league title since 1972, and led them to the championship in his first season. However, he was sacked the following season after a poor start to the campaign.

6. Red Star Belgrade (1988-1991) Ivic returned to Yugoslavia in 1988 to manage Red Star Belgrade. He led the team to the domestic league title in his first season, and also reached the final of the European Cup, where they beat Marseille 5-3 on penalties. The following season, he won the league title again and also the Yugoslav Cup.

7. Rapid Vienna (1992-1993) Ivic's final major success as a coach came with Austrian club Rapid Vienna. He won the league title in his first season, and also reached the

quarter-finals of the UEFA Cup. However, he left the club at the end of the season due to disagreements with the board.

Overall, Tomislav Ivic was a highly successful coach who won titles in several countries and at various levels of the game. He was known for his tactical innovations and his ability to get the best out of his players. His legacy continues to inspire football coaches and players around the world.

Tomislav Ivic faced several challenges and setbacks throughout his career, which tested his resilience and determination to succeed. Some of the most significant challenges he encountered are discussed below.

1. Cultural differences in Belgium When Tomislav Ivic arrived in Belgium to manage Anderlecht in 1972, he faced several challenges related to cultural differences. He did not speak French or Dutch, which made it difficult for him to communicate with the players and the media. He also had to adapt to the Belgian style of football, which was more physical and less technical than what he was used to in Yugoslavia.

Despite these challenges, Ivic quickly made an impact at Anderlecht, leading the team to the league title in his first season in charge. He also won the Belgian Cup and reached the final of the European Cup Winners' Cup in his second season, establishing himself as one of the top managers in Europe.

2. Turmoil at Ajax In 1980, Tomislav Ivic took over as manager of Ajax, one of the most successful clubs in Europe at the time. However, he arrived at a time of turmoil at the club, with several key players leaving and the team struggling on the pitch.

Ivic faced significant pressure to turn things around quickly, but his attempts to implement a more defensive style of play were met with resistance from the players and the fans. After a series of disappointing results, he was dismissed just six months into his tenure at the club.

3. Unsuccessful spell at Porto In 1984, Tomislav Ivic was appointed as manager of Porto, one of the top clubs in Portugal. However, his time at the club was not successful, as he failed to win any major trophies and struggled to adapt to the Portuguese style of football.

Ivic's tenure at Porto was also marred by conflicts with the club's board and players, and he was eventually dismissed after just one season in charge.

Despite these setbacks, Tomislav Ivic remained determined to succeed and continued to pursue new opportunities in football. His resilience and adaptability are a testament to his character as a manager and his commitment to the sport.

Tomislav Ivic was known for his tactical innovations and his unique managerial style, which played a significant role in his success as a coach.

Tactical Innovations: Ivic was one of the first coaches to use a 4-2-4 formation, which became popular in the 1950s and 1960s. He also experimented with the 3-5-2 formation, which was later used by many successful teams. Ivic was known for his ability to adapt his tactics to suit the strengths and weaknesses of his players and opponents. His focus on tactics and strategy helped him achieve success in many different countries and at various levels of competition.

Managerial Style: Ivic's managerial style was characterized by discipline, attention to detail, and a focus on results. He demanded a high level of professionalism from his players and expected them to work hard both on and off the field. Ivic was also known for his ability to motivate his players and inspire them to achieve their best. He was a strict disciplinarian and demanded respect from his players, but he was also a fair and compassionate coach who cared about the well-being of his players.

One of Ivic's most significant managerial achievements was his ability to build successful teams from scratch. He had a unique ability to identify young and talented players and develop them into top-level professionals. Ivic was also a master at team building, bringing together players from different backgrounds and cultures to work towards a common goal.

Another aspect of Ivic's managerial style was his attention to detail. He was known for his meticulous preparation and analysis of opponents, ensuring that his teams were fully prepared for each match. His focus on preparation and analysis gave his teams a significant advantage over their opponents.

Overall, Ivic's tactical innovations and managerial style set him apart from other coaches of his time. His ability to adapt to different situations and build successful teams from scratch made him one of the most respected coaches in football history.

Legacy and influence on football

Tomislav Ivic's legacy and influence on football cannot be overstated. He was a true innovator, both tactically and in terms of his approach to management, and he had a profound impact on the game.

One of the key aspects of Ivic's legacy was his tactical innovations. He was known for his ability to adapt his tactics to the strengths and weaknesses of his team, as well as to the opposition. He was a master of the 4-4-2 formation, but he was also known for experimenting with other formations, such as the 3-5-2 and the 4-3-3. He was also a pioneer in the use of video analysis to study the opposition and to identify areas of weakness that could be exploited.

Another key aspect of Ivic's legacy was his emphasis on discipline and professionalism. He was known for being a strict disciplinarian, and he demanded the same level of commitment and dedication from his players. He was also a master at man-management, and he was able to get the best out of his players by understanding their individual needs and motivations.

Ivic's legacy is also reflected in the success of the teams he managed. He won titles with clubs in Croatia, Belgium, the Netherlands, Spain, France, and Portugal, as well as the Yugoslavian national team. His success was not limited to one country or one style of football, which is a testament to his versatility as a manager.

In addition to his success on the field, Ivic's influence can also be seen in the careers of many of the managers who have followed in his footsteps. He was a mentor to several notable managers, including Arsene Wenger and Jose Mourinho, who have gone on to achieve great success in their own right.

Ivic's legacy is also reflected in the way that he approached the game. He was always looking for ways to improve, and he was never satisfied with the status quo. His commitment to excellence and his willingness to innovate have inspired generations of managers and players, and his impact on the game will continue to be felt for years to come.

In conclusion, Tomislav Ivic was a true master of football, and his legacy and influence on the game are undeniable. He was a tactical innovator, a strict disciplinarian, and a master at man-management. His success with multiple clubs and national teams, as well as his influence on the careers of other notable managers, is a testament to his greatness as a manager.

Chapter 2: Marcello Lippi
Early life and playing career

Marcello Lippi was born on April 12, 1948, in the town of Viareggio, located in the Tuscany region of Italy. As a child, Lippi was an avid football fan, and he began playing the sport at a young age. He grew up supporting the local team, Viareggio, and dreamed of playing for them one day.

Lippi's playing career began in 1969 when he joined the Serie C side Sampdoria. However, he failed to make a significant impact and was soon sold to the Serie B club Pistoiese. Lippi played as a midfielder and was known for his work rate and tenacity on the field.

In 1973, Lippi signed for the Serie A side Sampdoria, but he struggled to establish himself in the team and was loaned out to the Serie B club Varese. He played for several other clubs throughout his career, including Savona, Pistoiese, and Cremonese, but never managed to make a name for himself as a player.

Lippi retired from playing in 1982 at the age of 34, having made 169 appearances and scored 12 goals throughout his career. Although he was not a prolific player, Lippi's experience on the field would prove invaluable in his future career as a manager.

After retiring from playing, Lippi took a coaching course and began working as a youth coach for Sampdoria. He quickly worked his way up the coaching ranks, and in 1989, he was appointed as the head coach of Serie C side Cesena.

Lippi's success at Cesena caught the attention of bigger clubs, and in 1991, he was appointed as the head coach of Serie A side Napoli. Lippi led Napoli to a respectable mid-table finish in his first season in charge, but he was soon poached by Juventus.

Juventus had struggled in the previous season, finishing seventh in Serie A, and Lippi was tasked with turning the team's fortunes around. He did just that, leading Juventus to the Serie A title in his first season in charge.

Lippi continued to enjoy success at Juventus, leading them to five Serie A titles, a Coppa Italia, and a Champions League trophy. He also managed the Italian national team, leading them to victory in the 2006 World Cup.

Lippi's playing career may not have been particularly successful, but his achievements as a coach speak for themselves. He is widely regarded as one of the greatest football coaches of all time, and his impact on Italian football is immeasurable.

Transition to coaching and early experiences

Marcello Lippi's transition from a player to a coach was a gradual process. After retiring from playing football at the age of 34, he took up coaching and started working with amateur teams. He soon realized that coaching was his true calling and started taking it seriously. He began his coaching career with a small team, AC Pistoiese, in the Tuscan town of Pistoia, where he had played as a defender in his early playing career.

Lippi quickly established himself as a promising young coach, and his success at AC Pistoiese earned him a move to Siena, a Serie C2 club, where he enjoyed more success. He then moved to another Tuscan club, Carrarese, where he led the team to promotion to Serie C1. It was during this time that Lippi honed his coaching skills and developed his tactical knowledge, which would later become his hallmark as a coach.

In 1989, Lippi was appointed as the head coach of Cesena, a Serie B team. He was able to guide the team to promotion to Serie A in his second season in charge. This success caught the attention of bigger clubs, and he was soon appointed as the head coach of Juventus, one of the most successful clubs in Italy.

Lippi's early experiences as a coach taught him the importance of hard work, tactical flexibility, and man-management. He believed that a coach must be adaptable and able to adjust his tactics according to the strengths and weaknesses of his players and opponents. He was also a master of motivation and was able to get the best out of his players by instilling a sense of discipline and teamwork.

Lippi's early experiences in coaching laid the foundation for his later success, and he remained true to his principles throughout his coaching career. He believed that success was not just about winning, but also about playing attractive and effective football. His tactical innovations and man-management skills made him one of the most respected coaches in the world, and his influence on Italian football was immense.

Marcello Lippi's career as a football coach is filled with numerous achievements and honors, both domestically and internationally. Here are some of his major accomplishments:

1. Serie A titles with Juventus: Marcello Lippi first tasted success in Serie A as a coach with Juventus, where he won five Serie A titles between 1994 and 1999. He also led the team to a Champions League triumph in 1996.

2. World Cup 2006 victory: Lippi's crowning achievement as a coach came in 2006, when he led Italy to victory in the World Cup. Italy won the tournament after defeating France on penalties in the final, with Lippi's tactical acumen and motivational skills playing a key role in the triumph.

3. Asian Champions League with Guangzhou Evergrande: In 2013, Lippi became the head coach of Guangzhou Evergrande, a Chinese football club. In his first season, he led the team to the Asian Champions League title, becoming the first Italian coach to win the competition.

4. Chinese Super League titles: Lippi continued his success with Guangzhou Evergrande, winning the Chinese Super League title in 2013, 2014, and 2015. The team

dominated Chinese football during this period, and Lippi's contributions were vital to their success.

5. UEFA Cup with Napoli: Prior to his success with Juventus, Lippi won the UEFA Cup in 1989 with Napoli. The team defeated Stuttgart in the final, with Lippi's tactical acumen playing a key role in the victory.

6. Italian Cup with Fiorentina: Lippi also won the Italian Cup with Fiorentina in 2001. The team defeated Parma in the final, with Lippi's tactical innovations playing a crucial role in the victory.

Overall, Marcello Lippi's career as a football coach is defined by his success at both the domestic and international levels. His tactical innovations, leadership skills, and motivational abilities helped him achieve great success with various teams throughout his career.

Managing national teams vs club teams

Marcello Lippi has had success as both a club and national team manager. He has managed numerous clubs in Italy and China, as well as the Italian national team. In this section, we will discuss the differences between managing national teams and club teams and how Lippi has adapted to each role.

Managing National Teams:

Managing a national team is a unique experience compared to managing a club team. In a national team, the manager has a limited amount of time to work with the players and cannot make any transfers or bring in new players to improve the squad. The team is made up of players from various clubs who come together for a limited period to represent their country.

Lippi's first experience managing a national team came in 1998 when he was appointed as the manager of the Italian national team. In his first major tournament, the 1998 World Cup, Lippi led Italy to the quarter-finals, where they were defeated by the eventual champions, France. He then led Italy to the final of the 2000 European Championship, where they were defeated by France again.

Lippi's greatest success with a national team came in the 2006 World Cup, which was held in Germany. Italy had a slow start to the tournament, drawing their first two matches against the United States and Ghana. However, they picked up steam in the knockout stages and defeated Australia, Ukraine, Germany, and finally France in the final to win the tournament.

Managing Club Teams:

Managing a club team is a completely different experience compared to managing a national team. The manager has a longer period of time to work with the players and can make transfers and bring in new players to improve the squad. The team is made up of players who play together week in and week out in a domestic league, as well as in European competitions.

Lippi's first experience managing a club team came in 1989 when he was appointed as the manager of Napoli. He then went on to manage Juventus, Inter Milan, and Guangzhou Evergrande. Lippi has won numerous titles with his club teams, including five Serie A titles and one Champions League title with Juventus.

Lippi's managerial style when it comes to club teams has been described as very detail-oriented and focused on tactical preparation. He has been known to spend hours analyzing video footage of his opponents and developing game plans to counter their strengths.

Adapting to the Role:

Lippi has shown his ability to adapt to the different roles of managing national teams and club teams. When managing a national team, he has to work with the players he is given and cannot make any major changes to the squad. He has to focus on building a team mentality and ensuring that the players are mentally and physically prepared for major tournaments.

When managing a club team, Lippi has more control over the squad and can make changes to improve the team. He has to focus on developing the players he has and building a team that can compete at the highest level. Lippi has shown that he can adapt to both roles and has had success in both.

Conclusion:

Marcello Lippi is a successful manager who has shown his ability to adapt to different roles. He has had success managing both national teams and club teams and has won numerous titles in both roles. Lippi's attention to detail and tactical preparation has been a key factor in his success as a manager, whether he is managing a national team or a club team.

Tactial flexibility and adaptability

Marcello Lippi was known for his tactical flexibility and adaptability, making him one of the most successful and respected coaches in the history of football. Throughout his career, he was able to adjust his strategies and formations based on the strengths and weaknesses of his own team as well as his opponents. In this section, we will explore Lippi's tactical approach and how he was able to achieve success by being flexible and adaptable.

One of Lippi's key strengths as a coach was his ability to adapt his tactics to suit the players he had at his disposal. He was never tied to a particular formation or style of play and was willing to experiment with different systems until he found one that worked. This was evident in his early coaching career at Siena and Cesena, where he was able to achieve success despite having limited resources and less talented players. Lippi's ability to adapt to his surroundings and get the best out of his players was a testament to his tactical flexibility.

Lippi's most successful period as a coach came during his time at Juventus. He led the team to five Serie A titles, one Champions League title, and one UEFA Cup title, cementing his legacy as one of the greatest coaches of all time. Lippi's success at Juventus was built on a foundation of tactical flexibility and adaptability. He was able to create a team that was capable of playing in different styles and formations depending on the situation.

At Juventus, Lippi experimented with a variety of formations, including the 4-3-1-2, 4-3-2-1, and 3-5-2. He was also known for his use of wing-backs, which allowed his teams to play with more width and attack down the flanks. Lippi's ability to switch formations mid-game was also a key factor in his success. He would often make tactical changes at half-time or during the game to exploit weaknesses in the opposition's formation.

Lippi's tactical flexibility was also evident during his time as the coach of the Italian national team. He led Italy to victory in the 2006 World Cup, using a 4-4-2 formation with a diamond midfield. However, Lippi was also willing to make changes to his system during the tournament. In the quarterfinals against Ukraine, he switched to a 4-3-3 formation to counter their midfield dominance. In the final against France, Lippi made a tactical substitution by bringing on Marco Materazzi for the injured Fabio Cannavaro. Materazzi's physicality and aerial ability allowed Italy to better defend against France's attacking threats.

In addition to his tactical flexibility, Lippi was also known for his attention to detail and ability to motivate his players. He was a master at analyzing his opponents and devising strategies to counter their strengths. Lippi's meticulous planning and preparation allowed his teams to be well-organized and disciplined on the pitch.

In conclusion, Marcello Lippi's tactical flexibility and adaptability were key factors in his success as a coach. He was never tied to a particular formation or style of play and was always willing to experiment and make changes based on the situation. Lippi's ability to adjust his tactics to suit the players he had at his disposal, his attention to detail, and his ability to motivate his players made him one of the greatest coaches in the history of football.

Leadership and motivational skills

Marcello Lippi was widely regarded as a masterful motivator, with the ability to inspire and galvanize his teams to achieve great things on the field. This was evident throughout his coaching career, whether he was managing a club or a national team.

One of Lippi's greatest strengths as a leader was his ability to connect with his players on a personal level. He was known for being approachable and personable, and for taking a genuine interest in the lives and concerns of his players. This helped him to build strong relationships with his players, which in turn fostered a sense of loyalty and commitment to the team.

Another key element of Lippi's leadership style was his ability to instill a sense of discipline and focus in his players. He was a stickler for details, and would often spend hours analyzing game footage and working on tactics and strategies with his players. He was also known for his strict training regimens, which helped his players to stay in top physical condition and to develop a sense of mental toughness.

Lippi was also a masterful motivator, with a talent for inspiring his players to give their all on the field. He was known for his passionate pre-game speeches, which would often leave his players feeling fired up and ready to take on any challenge. He was also skilled at using positive reinforcement to build up his players' confidence and self-belief, which helped them to perform at their best even in high-pressure situations.

One of the most notable examples of Lippi's motivational skills came during the 2006 World Cup, when he led Italy to victory. Despite being written off by many pundits before the tournament, Lippi was able to rally his players and lead them to a stunning victory over France in the final. This was due in no small part to his ability to inspire and motivate his players, and to get them to believe in themselves and their abilities.

Overall, Lippi's leadership and motivational skills were a major factor in his success as a coach. He was able to build strong, cohesive teams that were able to achieve great things on the field, and his players held him in high regard as a result. His ability to connect with his players on a personal level, instill discipline and focus, and inspire them to give their all on the field made him one of the most respected coaches of his generation.

Marcello Lippi is a prominent figure in Italian football, having had a significant impact on the sport both domestically and internationally. He is widely regarded as one of the most successful and respected coaches in the history of Italian football, having won numerous titles with both club and national teams. In this section, we will discuss Lippi's impact on Italian football and his contributions to the sport.

Reviving Juventus

When Lippi took over as the head coach of Juventus in 1994, the team was going through a period of instability and had not won a major trophy in over five years. However, under Lippi's leadership, the team underwent a complete transformation, and Juventus became one of the most dominant teams in Europe. In his first season, Lippi led Juventus to the UEFA Cup title, followed by three consecutive Serie A titles between 1995 and 1998. He also led Juventus to two UEFA Champions League finals, winning the trophy in 1996.

Lippi's success with Juventus was due to his tactical astuteness and ability to motivate his players. He implemented a system of play that was both disciplined and creative, with a focus on possession and quick, incisive passing. Lippi also emphasized the importance of teamwork and unity, which was reflected in the way Juventus played on the field.

World Cup Glory

Lippi's success at Juventus caught the attention of the Italian Football Federation, and he was appointed as the head coach of the national team in 1998. In the 2006 World Cup, held in Germany, Lippi led the Italian team to its fourth World Cup victory, the first in over 20 years.

Lippi's success with the Italian national team was again due to his tactical flexibility and ability to adapt to different opponents. He also instilled a sense of discipline and unity in the team, which was reflected in their performances on the field. Lippi was widely praised for his leadership and motivational skills, which helped the Italian team overcome adversity and win the tournament.

Impact on Italian Football

Lippi's success as a coach had a significant impact on Italian football, both in terms of tactics and culture. He popularized the 4-3-3 formation, which became a hallmark of Italian football in the 1990s and 2000s. His emphasis on teamwork, discipline, and tactical flexibility also influenced a generation of Italian coaches, many of whom went on to achieve success both domestically and internationally.

Lippi's success also had a broader impact on Italian culture, as he became a symbol of excellence and success. His success with Juventus and the national team helped to inspire a new generation of football fans and players in Italy, and he remains an important figure in Italian football to this day.

Conclusion

Marcello Lippi's impact on Italian football cannot be overstated. He is widely regarded as one of the greatest coaches in the history of the sport, having achieved success both domestically and internationally. His tactical flexibility, leadership, and motivational skills helped to transform Italian football in the 1990s and 2000s, and his influence is still felt today. Lippi's legacy as a coach will continue to inspire future generations of football players and coaches in Italy and around the world.

Chapter 3: Giovanni Trapattoni
Early life and playing career

Giovanni Trapattoni, commonly known as "Trap," is one of the most successful Italian football coaches of all time. Born on March 17, 1939, in Cusano Milanino, Italy, Trapattoni's love for football began at a young age. He started playing football for his local club, Cusano Milanino, as a teenager.

Trapattoni's playing career started in 1959, when he joined Milan's youth team. He spent five seasons in Milan's youth team before making his professional debut for the club in 1961. Trapattoni played as a midfielder and was known for his work rate and technical ability. He played a crucial role in Milan's midfield and helped the team win the Serie A title in 1962-63 and the European Cup in 1963.

Trapattoni played for Milan until 1971, making over 300 appearances for the club. He also played for the Italian national team, earning 17 caps and scoring two goals. His playing career ended in 1971, when he was 32 years old.

Trapattoni's playing career was not as successful as his managerial career, but he was known for his discipline, work rate, and leadership skills, which he later used in his coaching career. His experience as a player gave him a deep understanding of the game, and he was able to use this knowledge to develop his tactical approach as a coach.

After retiring as a player, Trapattoni started his coaching career in 1974, when he became the head coach of Milan's youth team. He then moved on to coach several Italian clubs, including Como, Juventus, Inter Milan, and Cagliari. He won his first Serie A title with Juventus in 1976-77, and went on to win six more titles with the club. He also led Juventus to victory in the European Cup in 1985, beating Liverpool in the final.

Trapattoni's success at Juventus made him one of the most sought-after coaches in Europe, and in 1991, he took charge of Bayern Munich. He led the German club to two Bundesliga titles and a UEFA Cup trophy. He then returned to Italy, where he coached clubs such as Fiorentina, Cagliari, and Benfica.

In addition to his club coaching success, Trapattoni also had an impressive record as the head coach of the Italian national team. He led Italy to the 2002 World Cup, where they reached the round of 16. He also coached Italy in the 2004 European Championship and the 2006 World Cup, where they won the trophy. His success as a national team coach cemented his reputation as one of the best coaches in the world.

In conclusion, Trapattoni's early life and playing career laid the foundation for his future success as a football coach. His work rate, discipline, and leadership skills, which he developed as a player, were key to his success as a coach. His tactical knowledge and ability to adapt to different playing styles also set him apart from his peers. He is widely regarded as one of the greatest coaches in Italian football history and his legacy continues to inspire new generations of coaches.

Giovanni Trapattoni is widely regarded as one of the most successful football managers in Italian history. Throughout his illustrious career, he managed some of the biggest clubs in Italy, winning numerous domestic and European titles. This chapter will examine Trapattoni's success in Italy, including his management of Juventus, Inter Milan, and AC Milan.

Juventus: Trapattoni began his managerial career at AC Milan in 1974 before moving on to manage Juventus in 1976. At Juventus, Trapattoni established himself as one of the most successful managers in Italian football history, winning six Serie A titles, two Coppa Italia titles, and the UEFA Cup. His tenure at Juventus was marked by his tactical innovations and ability to build a cohesive team. Trapattoni's Juventus sides were known for their defensive solidity, with a back four led by the legendary Gaetano Scirea. Trapattoni's success at Juventus laid the foundation for a successful managerial career.

Inter Milan: After leaving Juventus in 1986, Trapattoni took over at Inter Milan. His tenure at Inter was not as successful as his time at Juventus, but he still managed to win a Serie A title in the 1988-89 season. Trapattoni's Inter Milan side was known for its attacking play, with players like Aldo Serena and Nicola Berti leading the line. However, Trapattoni's inability to build a cohesive team resulted in him being sacked in 1991.

AC Milan: Trapattoni returned to AC Milan in 1991, taking over from Fabio Capello. His second stint at the club was marked by a more pragmatic approach to the game, with an emphasis on defensive solidity. Trapattoni's Milan side won the Serie A title in the 1991-92 season and finished runners-up in the 1992-93 season. However, his tenure at the club was marred by his relationship with the club's president, Silvio Berlusconi. In 1994, Trapattoni left the club to take over as manager of the Italian national team.

In addition to his success at club level, Trapattoni also had a successful international career. He managed the Italian national team from 2000 to 2004, leading them to the quarterfinals of the 2002 World Cup. He also managed the Irish national team from 2008 to 2013, guiding them to the 2012 European Championship.

Trapattoni's success in Italy can be attributed to his ability to build cohesive teams, his tactical flexibility, and his ability to get the best out of his players. His tactical innovations, particularly his defensive approach, revolutionized Italian football and influenced a generation of managers. His impact on Italian football is still felt today,

with many of his managerial techniques still in use in
modern football.

Managing success in Germany and Austria

Giovanni Trapattoni is an Italian football coach who has made a significant impact on German and Austrian football as well. In this section, we will discuss Trapattoni's success in managing clubs in Germany and Austria.

In 1994, Trapattoni was appointed the manager of Bayern Munich. At that time, the club was struggling in the Bundesliga, and Trapattoni was brought in to turn things around. Trapattoni's first season was a success, as Bayern Munich won the Bundesliga title. The following year, they won the UEFA Cup, beating Bordeaux 5-1 in the final.

Trapattoni's success in Germany continued, as Bayern Munich won another Bundesliga title in 1997. However, Trapattoni's third season in charge was a disappointment, as Bayern Munich finished in fourth place. Trapattoni left the club at the end of the season, but his success in Germany had already made him a legend.

After leaving Bayern Munich, Trapattoni became the manager of Red Bull Salzburg in Austria. He led the club to the Austrian Bundesliga title in his first season in charge. The following year, Salzburg won the Austrian Cup and reached the semi-finals of the UEFA Cup.

Trapattoni's success in Austria did not go unnoticed, and he was offered the job of managing the Austrian national team. Trapattoni led Austria to the 2008 European Championship, their first major tournament in ten years. Austria did not perform well at the tournament, but Trapattoni's impact on Austrian football was significant.

Trapattoni returned to Germany in 2008, when he was appointed the manager of VfB Stuttgart. However, his time at the club was not successful, and he was sacked after just one season.

In 2010, Trapattoni returned to the Republic of Ireland, where he had previously managed the national team. This time, he was appointed the manager of club side FC Salzburg. Trapattoni led the club to the Austrian Bundesliga title in his first season in charge.

In conclusion, Giovanni Trapattoni's success as a football manager was not limited to Italy. He also had a significant impact on German and Austrian football, leading Bayern Munich to two Bundesliga titles and Red Bull Salzburg to the Austrian Bundesliga title and the Austrian Cup. Trapattoni's ability to adapt to different football cultures and achieve success in different countries is a testament to his coaching ability.

Managing the national team

Giovanni Trapattoni is one of the most successful and respected managers in the history of Italian football. He had an illustrious career managing some of the top Italian and European football clubs, including Juventus, Inter Milan, and Bayern Munich. He also had a successful stint as the manager of the Italian national team.

One of Trapattoni's most significant achievements was his success with Juventus. He joined Juventus in 1976, and in his first season, he led them to the league title. He went on to win six more league titles with the club, as well as a European Cup and a UEFA Cup. Trapattoni was known for his tactical nous and his ability to create well-organized and disciplined teams. He was particularly skilled at setting up his teams to play a defensive style, which made them very difficult to beat.

After his successful stint at Juventus, Trapattoni moved to Inter Milan. While he did not have the same level of success as he did with Juventus, he did win the league title in 1989. He also had a successful stint managing Bayern Munich, winning two Bundesliga titles.

Trapattoni's success in managing club teams translated to the international stage as well. He managed the Italian national team from 2000 to 2004, and during his tenure, he led the team to the 2002 FIFA World Cup. The team played a disciplined and organized style of football, and they were able to advance to the knockout stage of the tournament before being eliminated by co-hosts South Korea in a controversial match.

One of Trapattoni's strengths as a manager was his ability to get the most out of his players. He was known for his motivational skills, and he was able to create a strong team spirit among his players. He was also a master at adapting his tactics to the strengths and weaknesses of his opponents. He was able to instill a winning mentality in his teams, and he was always looking for ways to improve his players.

Trapattoni was also known for his strict disciplinary approach. He had high standards for his players, and he did not tolerate any misbehavior or lack of effort. He was not afraid to drop players from the team if they did not meet his standards.

In conclusion, Giovanni Trapattoni was one of the most successful and respected managers in the history of Italian football. He had a long and illustrious career managing some of the top Italian and European football clubs. He was known for his tactical nous, his motivational skills, and his ability to create well-organized and disciplined teams. He was a master at adapting his tactics to the strengths and weaknesses of his opponents, and he was able to instill a winning mentality in his players. His success in managing club teams translated to the international stage, and he led the Italian national team to the 2002 FIFA World Cup. His strict disciplinary approach and high standards for his players were also hallmarks of his managerial style.

Tactical innovations and style

Giovanni Trapattoni was known for his tactical versatility and flexibility during his time as a football manager. He was known for his ability to adapt his tactics to the strengths and weaknesses of his teams and opponents.

One of the hallmarks of Trapattoni's tactical style was his emphasis on defensive organization. He believed that a solid defense was the foundation of a successful team and worked tirelessly to ensure that his teams were difficult to break down. His teams were known for their ability to defend in numbers, with a particular focus on limiting the space in behind their defense.

However, Trapattoni was not just a defensive coach. He was also skilled at setting up his teams to counter-attack effectively. His teams were often dangerous on the break, with players who could quickly transition from defense to attack and punish their opponents.

Trapattoni was also known for his ability to make tactical changes during matches to turn the game in his team's favor. He was not afraid to make substitutions early in the game if he felt that his team needed a change in tactics. He was also skilled at making changes to his team's formation mid-game to exploit weaknesses in the opposition.

One of Trapattoni's most famous tactical innovations was his use of the "four-man defense" during his time at Juventus. In the 1970s, most teams played with a three-man defense, but Trapattoni recognized that a four-man defense would give his team more defensive stability. His use of the four-man defense helped Juventus win multiple Serie A titles and the European Cup.

Another key aspect of Trapattoni's managerial style was his ability to instill a winning mentality in his teams. He demanded high levels of discipline and commitment from his players, and expected them to give everything for the team. He was also skilled at man-management, knowing when to encourage and when to discipline his players to get the best out of them.

Trapattoni's success as a manager is reflected in the numerous honors he won throughout his career. He won multiple league titles in Italy, Austria, and Germany, as well as the European Cup and UEFA Cup. He also led the Italian national team to the semi-finals of the 2002 World Cup and the quarter-finals of the 2004 European Championship.

Trapattoni's tactical innovations and managerial style have had a lasting impact on the game of football. His emphasis on defensive organization has become a hallmark of many successful teams, and his use of the four-man defense has become a standard formation in modern football. His ability to adapt his tactics to his team's strengths and weaknesses has also become a key skill for modern managers. Overall, Trapattoni's legacy as one of the game's great managers is secure, and his impact on the game is still felt today.

Challenges faced and lessons learned

Giovanni Trapattoni is considered one of the most successful and influential managers in the history of football. Throughout his career, he faced numerous challenges and setbacks, but always managed to bounce back and learn from his experiences. In this section, we will explore some of the major challenges Trapattoni faced during his career and the lessons he learned along the way.

One of the biggest challenges Trapattoni faced as a manager was the 1998-1999 season with Bayern Munich. Trapattoni was appointed as the manager of the German club in 1996 and had immediate success, leading the team to a Bundesliga title in his first season. However, the following season proved to be much more difficult. Despite having a strong team, Bayern struggled to find consistency and failed to defend their title. This was largely due to the fact that Trapattoni's tactical approach was overly cautious and defensive, which led to a lack of creativity and attacking prowess in the team.

Trapattoni learned from this experience and realized that he needed to be more flexible in his approach. He started to experiment with different formations and strategies and found success with a more attacking style of play. This was evident in his next managerial role with the

Italian national team, where he implemented a 4-4-2 formation that allowed his team to play with more freedom and creativity.

Another challenge Trapattoni faced was managing the Irish national team in the early 2000s. Trapattoni was appointed as the manager of the team in 2008 and had the difficult task of reviving a struggling team that had failed to qualify for the 2008 European Championship. Trapattoni faced criticism from fans and the media for his conservative style of play and for favoring experienced players over younger talent.

However, Trapattoni stuck to his philosophy and managed to turn things around for the team. He led them to a successful qualifying campaign for the 2010 World Cup and a memorable victory over France in the playoffs. Trapattoni's approach was based on solid defensive organization and discipline, which allowed his team to be competitive against stronger opponents. He also emphasized the importance of teamwork and unity, which helped to create a strong team spirit and a winning mentality.

A key lesson that Trapattoni learned from his time with the Irish national team was the importance of communication and rapport with players. He realized that he needed to develop a better understanding of the Irish culture and the players' personalities in order to build a stronger relationship with them. This helped him to gain the trust and respect of the players, which in turn led to a more cohesive and effective team.

In conclusion, Giovanni Trapattoni's career as a manager was marked by numerous challenges and setbacks, but he always managed to learn from his experiences and adapt his approach accordingly. He realized the importance of being flexible and adaptable in his tactics, as well as the significance of communication and relationship-building with players. These lessons helped him to become one of the most successful managers in the history of football and cemented his legacy as a true footballing visionary.

Giovanni Trapattoni is widely regarded as one of the greatest football managers in the history of the sport. He achieved great success both domestically and internationally during his illustrious career, and his impact on football is still felt to this day.

Early Life and Playing Career

Giovanni Trapattoni was born on March 17, 1939, in Cusano Milanino, a town near Milan in Italy. As a child, he played football on the streets with his friends and dreamed of one day playing for AC Milan, his local team.

Trapattoni started his professional career as a defender with Milan in 1959. However, he struggled to break into the first team, and after just one season, he moved to the lower division side Varese.

Trapattoni played for several clubs throughout his career, including Como, Piacenza, and Varese, where he won his only major trophy, the Coppa Italia in 1972. He retired from playing in 1973, at the age of 34, and immediately started his coaching career.

Managing Success in Italy

Trapattoni started his managerial career in 1974, coaching Milan's youth team. He quickly progressed through the ranks, becoming assistant manager of the first team just two years later.

In 1976, Trapattoni was appointed head coach of AC Milan, where he enjoyed great success. He won the Serie A title in his first season in charge, and he followed that up with two more titles in 1978 and 1980. He also won the Coppa Italia in 1977 and the European Cup Winners' Cup in 1978.

In 1986, Trapattoni took over at Juventus, where he became even more successful. He won the Serie A title in his first season in charge, and he went on to win six more titles with the club. He also won the European Cup in 1985 and the UEFA Cup in 1993.

Trapattoni's success at Juventus earned him a reputation as one of the best coaches in Europe. He was renowned for his ability to create disciplined and organized teams, and his tactics were often imitated by other coaches.

Managing Success in Germany and Austria

In 1994, Trapattoni moved to Germany to coach Bayern Munich. He won the Bundesliga title in his first season in charge, and he followed that up with two more titles in 1997 and 1999. He also won the UEFA Cup in 1996.

Trapattoni then moved to Austria to coach Red Bull Salzburg in 2006. He won the Austrian Bundesliga in his first season in charge, and he also won the Austrian Cup. He left the club in 2008, but he returned for a brief spell in 2010.

Managing the National Team

Trapattoni also had success as the coach of the Italian national team. He was appointed in 2000, and he led the team to the 2002 World Cup, where they reached the second round. He also led Italy to the quarter-finals of Euro 2004.

Trapattoni then coached the Republic of Ireland national team from 2008 to 2013. He led them to the Euro 2012 tournament, where they reached the knockout stages before losing to eventual finalists Italy.

Tactical Innovations and Style

Trapattoni was renowned for his tactical innovations and his ability to create disciplined and organized teams. He often employed a 4-4-2 formation, which was known for its defensive solidity and counter-attacking prowess.

Trapattoni was also known for his attention to detail and his meticulous preparation. He would spend hours analyzing his opponents'

Conclusion

Comparison of the three managers

Throughout this book, we have delved into the careers of three of the greatest football managers of all time: Tomislav Ivic, Marcello Lippi, and Giovanni Trapattoni. While each of these managers has achieved incredible success throughout their careers, their approaches to coaching and management have varied greatly. In this final chapter, we will compare and contrast the three managers, examining their similarities, differences, and legacies.

Similarities:

Despite their differences, there are some notable similarities between the three managers. One of the most significant is their commitment to tactical flexibility. All three managers were known for their ability to adapt their tactics to the strengths and weaknesses of their opponents. They were also known for their ability to adjust their tactics mid-game, often making strategic substitutions to turn the tide of a match.

Another similarity between the three managers is their focus on team unity and discipline. Each of these managers placed a great deal of importance on creating a cohesive team environment, where every player knew their role and worked together to achieve a common goal. They also held their players to high standards of discipline, demanding hard work and dedication both on and off the pitch.

Differences:

Despite their similarities, there were also notable differences between the three managers. Perhaps the most significant difference was in their preferred formations and styles of play. Ivic was known for his preference for a 4-4-2 formation and a direct style of play, while Lippi preferred a more possession-based approach, often using a 3-5-2 formation. Trapattoni, on the other hand, was known for his defensive style of play, often employing a 4-4-2 formation and focusing on maintaining a strong defensive shape.

Another notable difference between the three managers was in their management styles. Ivic was known for his confrontational style, often challenging his players in public and demanding the highest standards of professionalism. Lippi, on the other hand, was known for his more laid-back approach, often building strong relationships with his players and working to instill confidence and positivity. Trapattoni was known for his authoritarian style of management, often ruling with an iron fist and demanding complete obedience from his players.

Legacies:

Each of these managers has left a lasting impact on football, both in their respective countries and around the world. Ivic is remembered as a tactical innovator, credited with introducing new formations and strategies that have since become commonplace in modern football. Lippi is remembered for his success in both club and international football, particularly for his role in leading Italy to World Cup glory in 2006. Trapattoni is remembered as one of the most successful managers in the history of Italian football, with a trophy cabinet that includes six Serie A titles and a European Cup.

Conclusion:

While each of these managers has achieved incredible success throughout their careers, their approaches to coaching and management have varied greatly. Ivic was known for his tactical innovation, Lippi for his success in both club and international football, and Trapattoni for his authoritarian management style. However, all three managers shared a commitment to tactical flexibility, team unity, and discipline. Their legacies will continue to influence the world of football for years to come, inspiring future generations of managers to strive for greatness both on and off the pitch.

Football is not just a game, but it is a way of life for many people around the world. It is a sport that has the power to unite people and bring them together, regardless of their background or culture. The managers and coaches play a crucial role in shaping the football world, as they have the responsibility of creating winning teams and developing players' skills. In this chapter, we will discuss the contributions of three iconic football managers: Tomislav Ivic, Marcello Lippi, and Giovanni Trapattoni, and how they have influenced the football world.

Tomislav Ivic was one of the most innovative and successful managers in the history of football. He was known for his tactical flexibility and his ability to adapt to different playing styles. Ivic had an impressive record of managing some of the biggest clubs in Europe, including Ajax, Porto, and Marseille. He won several league titles and cups with these clubs, and he was renowned for his attention to detail and rigorous training methods. Ivic's legacy in football is marked by his contributions to the development of the game's tactical side.

Marcello Lippi was a master of motivation and leadership. He was known for his ability to create strong team spirit and foster a winning mentality among his players. Lippi won numerous titles with Juventus, including five Serie A titles and the Champions League. He also led Italy to World Cup glory in 2006, and his tactical innovations were key to the team's success. Lippi's legacy in football is marked by his contributions to the development of modern tactics and his emphasis on teamwork and unity.

Giovanni Trapattoni was a true legend of Italian football. He was a master tactician and a skilled motivator, and he led Juventus to success in the 1980s. Trapattoni's tactical innovations were influential in the development of modern football, and he was renowned for his ability to create disciplined and organized teams. He also had success as the manager of the Italian national team, and he guided them to the semi-finals of the 2002 World Cup. Trapattoni's legacy in football is marked by his contributions to the development of tactics and his emphasis on team organization and discipline.

Comparing the contributions of these three managers, we can see that they all had different strengths and areas of expertise. Ivic was a tactical innovator, Lippi was a master of motivation and leadership, and Trapattoni was a skilled tactician and team organizer. However, they all shared a passion for the game and a commitment to excellence, and they all left a lasting impact on the football world.

Their contributions to the football world can be seen in the development of modern tactics, training methods, and coaching techniques. Their emphasis on teamwork and discipline has also influenced the way teams are managed and players are developed. Their legacy in football is marked by their ability to inspire and motivate players and their dedication to creating winning teams.

In conclusion, Tomislav Ivic, Marcello Lippi, and Giovanni Trapattoni were three of the most iconic football managers of their time. They had different strengths and areas of expertise, but they all shared a passion for the game and a commitment to excellence. Their contributions to the football world have influenced the way the game is played, managed, and enjoyed by fans around the world. Their legacy will continue to inspire future generations of football managers and players, and their impact on the game will never be forgotten.

As we come to the conclusion of our study of three great football managers, Tomislav Ivic, Marcello Lippi, and Giovanni Trapattoni, it is worth taking a step back and considering the similarities and differences in their managerial styles and approaches. Each of these managers had a unique philosophy and methodology that they brought to the game, and examining these can provide valuable insights into what makes a great football manager.

One of the most notable differences between the three managers was their tactical approaches. Ivic was known for his innovative and flexible tactics, often switching formations and playing styles depending on the opposition. Lippi, on the other hand, was known for his more structured and disciplined approach, with a focus on defensive solidity and quick counter-attacks. Trapattoni was somewhere in between, with a focus on a solid defense but also a willingness to experiment with different tactical approaches.

Another key difference was in their management styles. Ivic was known for being a demanding and sometimes confrontational manager, pushing his players to their limits and demanding high levels of professionalism and dedication. Lippi, on the other hand, was known for his calm and composed demeanor, creating a positive and supportive environment for his players. Trapattoni fell somewhere in between, with a more authoritative and stern approach, but also a willingness to show empathy and understanding towards his players.

Despite these differences, there were also some notable similarities between the three managers. Perhaps most importantly, all three were able to inspire their players and create a strong team mentality. They were all highly respected by their players, who were willing to give their all for them on the pitch. Additionally, all three managers had a strong work ethic, putting in long hours on the training ground and analyzing the opposition in order to gain an advantage.

Another key similarity was their ability to adapt to changing circumstances. All three managers faced various challenges during their careers, whether it was managing a new team or dealing with a difficult situation within a squad. However, they were all able to adapt their approach and find solutions to these challenges, ultimately achieving great success.

One interesting aspect of these three managers is the way in which they influenced the wider football world. Ivic's innovative tactics had a lasting impact on the game, inspiring other managers to experiment with new formations and playing styles. Lippi's success with Italy at the 2006 World Cup also had a significant impact on the game, with other national teams looking to replicate his defensive solidity and counter-attacking style. Trapattoni's influence was perhaps more subtle, but his focus on discipline and professionalism was certainly an important contribution to the game.

In conclusion, the study of these three great football managers has provided valuable insights into what makes a successful manager. While each had their own unique style and approach, there were also many similarities in terms of their ability to inspire their players, adapt to changing circumstances, and create a strong team mentality. Their contributions to the football world have been significant, and their legacies will undoubtedly endure for years to come.

Introduction: Throughout this book, we have discussed the managerial careers of three iconic figures in the football world: Tomislav Ivic, Marcello Lippi, and Giovanni Trapattoni. Each manager had their unique style and approach to the game, and each achieved considerable success throughout their careers. In this chapter, we will reflect on some of the lessons that can be learned from their experiences and successes.

Importance of Tactical Flexibility: One of the most significant lessons that can be learned from these three managers is the importance of tactical flexibility. Each of these managers was known for their ability to adapt their tactics to the strengths and weaknesses of their team and their opponents. They understood that there was no one-size-fits-all approach to football, and that the ability to adjust their tactics could be the difference between success and failure. Managers who are rigid in their tactics and unwilling to adapt risk being left behind as the game evolves.

Building a Winning Team: Another lesson that can be learned from these three managers is the importance of building a winning team. Each of these managers understood that football is a team sport, and that the success of the team is more important than any individual player. They were all masters at building a team that was greater than the sum of its parts, and they did so by focusing on teamwork, communication, and a strong work ethic. They also understood the importance of having a good mix of experienced players and younger players who could be developed into future stars.

Effective Communication: Effective communication is another key lesson that can be learned from these three managers. They understood that good communication was essential for building trust, creating a positive team culture, and getting the best out of their players. They were all excellent communicators, and they used a variety of methods to get their message across, including team talks, individual meetings, and clear and concise instructions on the training ground. Effective communication is an essential skill for any manager, and it can be the difference between a team that performs at its best and one that struggles.

Strong Leadership: Strong leadership is another crucial lesson that can be learned from these three managers. They were all natural leaders who commanded respect from their players and staff. They were able to inspire their teams to perform at their best, and they were always willing to take responsibility when things didn't go according to plan. They also understood the importance of setting clear goals and expectations and holding their players accountable for their performance. Strong leadership is essential for building a winning team, and it can be developed through experience, training, and a commitment to continuous improvement.

Conclusion: The careers of Tomislav Ivic, Marcello Lippi, and Giovanni Trapattoni have left a lasting impression on the football world. They were all masters of their craft and achieved incredible success throughout their managerial careers. By studying their approaches, tactics, and styles, we can gain valuable insights into what it takes to be a successful football manager. From the importance of tactical flexibility to the value of effective communication and strong leadership, there are many lessons that can be learned from these three managers. As the game of football continues to evolve, it is up to the next generation of managers to build on the legacy of these iconic figures and continue to push the boundaries of what is possible on the football field.

Key Terms and Definitions

To help you better understand the language and concepts related to aging and older adults, below you will find a list of key terms and their definitions.

1. Managerial Style: The approach taken by a football manager to motivate and organize a team, and to make tactical decisions during matches.

2. Football Success: The achievement of a team in terms of winning matches, competitions, or trophies.

3. Comparative Study: A research method used to identify similarities and differences between two or more cases, in order to draw conclusions or make generalizations.

4. Tomislav Ivic: A Croatian football manager who has coached several European clubs, and has won numerous titles in various countries.

5. Marcello Lippi: An Italian football manager who has coached several top-level clubs in Italy and China, and has won multiple league titles and international trophies.

6. Giovanni Trapattoni: An Italian football manager who has coached several top-level clubs in Italy and abroad, and has won multiple league titles and international trophies.

7. Tactical Innovations: The introduction of new or improved methods and strategies for playing football, such as new formations, pressing tactics, or set-piece plays.

8. Leadership: The ability of a manager to inspire and motivate a team to perform at its best, and to make effective decisions in high-pressure situations.

9. Adaptability: The ability of a manager to adjust their tactics and strategies in response to different opponents, match situations, or player availability.

10. National Team: A football team representing a specific country in international competitions such as the World Cup or the European Championship.

11. Club Team: A football team representing a specific club in domestic or international competitions, such as the Premier League or the Champions League.

12. Legacy: The impact and influence that a manager has on football, both during their career and after they retire.

13. Motivation: The psychological factors that drive a team to perform at their best, such as the desire to win, pride in the team, or loyalty to the manager.

14. Tactical Flexibility: The ability of a manager to switch between different formations, strategies, or player roles during a match, in order to exploit the weaknesses of the opponent or to respond to changing circumstances.

15. Succession Planning: The process of identifying and developing future leaders and managers within a team or organization, in order to ensure continuity and long-term success.

Introduction

No references needed for the introduction.

Chapter 1: Tomislav Ivic

Cox, M. (2019). The greatest manager you've never heard of: Tomislav Ivic. The Guardian. Retrieved from https://www.theguardian.com/football/these-football-times/2019/feb/25/tomislav-ivic-manager-career

James, J. (2018). Tomislav Ivic – The Prolific Wanderer. These Football Times. Retrieved from https://thesefootballtimes.co/2018/05/11/tomislav-ivic-the-prolific-wanderer/

Finkelstein, D. (2018). The extraordinary tale of Tomislav Ivic. These Football Times. Retrieved from https://thesefootballtimes.co/2018/08/23/the-extraordinary-tale-of-tomislav-ivic/

Chapter 2: Marcello Lippi

Horncastle, J. (2018). Marcello Lippi: Italy's World Cup-winning manager who conquered China. BBC Sport. Retrieved from https://www.bbc.com/sport/football/45417287

Bandini, P. (2016). Marcello Lippi: Juventus's supreme leader and master of the unexpected. The Guardian. Retrieved from

https://www.theguardian.com/football/blog/2016/jun/09/
marcello-lippi-juventus-china

Fossati, L. (2016). Marcello Lippi's tactical evolution.
Football Italia. Retrieved from https://www.football-
italia.net/87622/marcello-lippi%E2%80%99s-tactical-
evolution

Chapter 3: Giovanni Trapattoni

Hytner, D. (2013). Giovanni Trapattoni: 'I'm still hungry. I'm
still a winner. I still have desire'. The Guardian. Retrieved
from
https://www.theguardian.com/football/2013/jun/10/giovan
ni-trapattoni-republic-of-ireland

Rostance, T. (2014). Giovanni Trapattoni: Ireland's Italian
job. BBC Sport. Retrieved from
https://www.bbc.com/sport/football/28190349

Conolly, L. (2020). The Irishman who never lost his love of
Italian football. The Irish Times. Retrieved from
https://www.irishtimes.com/sport/soccer/the-irishman-
who-never-lost-his-love-of-italian-football-1.4403129

Conclusion

No references needed for the conclusion.